Dogs on Duty

Service Dogs

by Marie Brandle

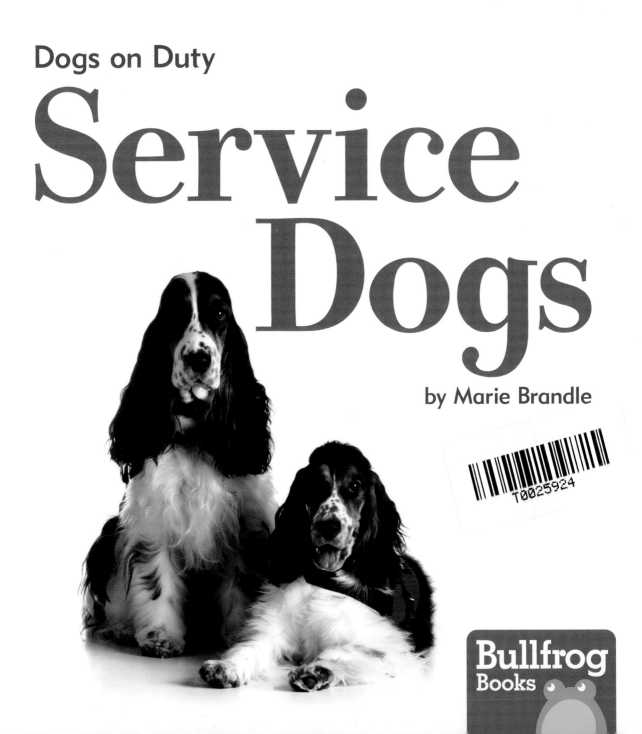

Ideas for Parents and Teachers

Bullfrog Books let children practice reading informational text at the earliest reading levels. Repetition, familiar words, and photo labels support early readers.

Before Reading
- Discuss the cover photo. What does it tell them?

- Look at the picture glossary together. Read and discuss the words.

Read the Book
- "Walk" through the book and look at the photos. Let the child ask questions. Point out the photo labels.

- Read the book to the child, or have him or her read independently.

After Reading
- Prompt the child to think more. Ask: Did you know about service dogs before reading this book? What more would you like to learn about them?

Bullfrog Books are published by Jump!
5357 Penn Avenue South
Minneapolis, MN 55419
www.jumplibrary.com

Library of Congress Cataloging-in-Publication Data

Names: Brandle, Marie, 1989– author.
Title: Service dogs / Marie Brandle.
Description: Minneapolis, MN: Jump!, Inc., [2022]
Series: Dogs on duty | Includes index.
Audience: Ages 5–8
Identifiers: LCCN 2021014967 (print)
LCCN 2021014968 (ebook)
ISBN 9781645279341 (hardcover)
ISBN 9781645279358 (paperback)
ISBN 9781645279365 (ebook)
Subjects: LCSH: Service dogs—Juvenile literature.
Classification: LCC HV1569.6 .B75 2022 (print)
LCC HV1569.6 (ebook) | DDC 636.7/0886—dc23
LC record available at https://lccn.loc.gov/2021014967
LC ebook record available at https://lccn.loc.gov/2021014968

Editor: Eliza Leahy
Designer: Molly Ballanger

Photo Credits: Pixel-Shot/Shutterstock, cover (girl); andresr/iStock, cover (dog); WilleeCole Photography/Shutterstock, 1; Michael Burrell/iStock, 3; Hyoung Chang/Getty, 4, 5; fstop123/iStock, 6–7, 23br; Huntstock/Getty, 8, 9, 23tr; Roman Chazov/Dreamstime, 10–11; Design Pics Inc/Alamy, 12; Mark Hunt/Getty, 13; Arterra/Getty, 14–15; MSPhotographic/Shutterstock, 16–17, 23tl; Shutterstock, 17, 23bl; SR Productions/Shutterstock, 18–19; adamkaz/iStock, 20–21; Africa Studio/Shutterstock, 22tl; Tom Kelley Archive/iStock, 22tr; Steve Clancy Photography/Getty, 22bl; tifonimages/iStock, 22br; Chuck Wagner/Shutterstock, 24.

Printed in the United States of America at Corporate Graphics in North Mankato, Minnesota.

Table of Contents

Helping Out

Scout has an important job.

He helps Matt get to school.
Scout is a service dog!

Service dogs are trained.

They help people.

How?

They do tasks.

Ed cannot hear.
Ruby paws at him.

Why?

The doorbell rang.

Ruby opens the door!

Ted cannot see.
Gus helps him find his way.

Morgan dropped the remote.

Bo helps.

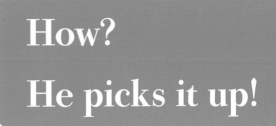

How?

He picks it up!

13

Mac helps Mia shop!

peanut
butter

Jake has a peanut allergy.

Lucy smells peanuts.

She barks.

This lets Jake know.

Many service dogs
wear vests.

Why?

This lets us know
they are working.

vest

SERVICE DOG

Service dogs help.
They are good
friends, too!

On the Job

Service dogs have many jobs. Take a look at some of them!

allergy alert dog
This dog's owner has a food allergy. She smells the food to make sure it is safe for her owner to eat.

guide dog
This dog's owner is blind. He guides his owner.

hearing dog
This dog's owner cannot hear. He alerts his owner when something makes noise, such as a doorbell.

mobility assistance dog
This dog's owner has a physical disability. She helps her owner get around and opens doors.

Picture Glossary

allergy
A condition that causes some people to become sick after eating, touching, or breathing something.

paws
Touches with a paw.

remote
A device for operating machines from a distance.

tasks
Pieces of work.

Index

To Learn More

Finding more information is as easy as 1, 2, 3.

❶ Go to www.factsurfer.com

❷ Enter "servicedogs" into the search box.

❸ Choose your book to see a list of websites.